CRAFTY IDEAS WITH JUNK

Melanie Rice

Illustrated by Lynne Farmer

Photography by Chris Fairclough

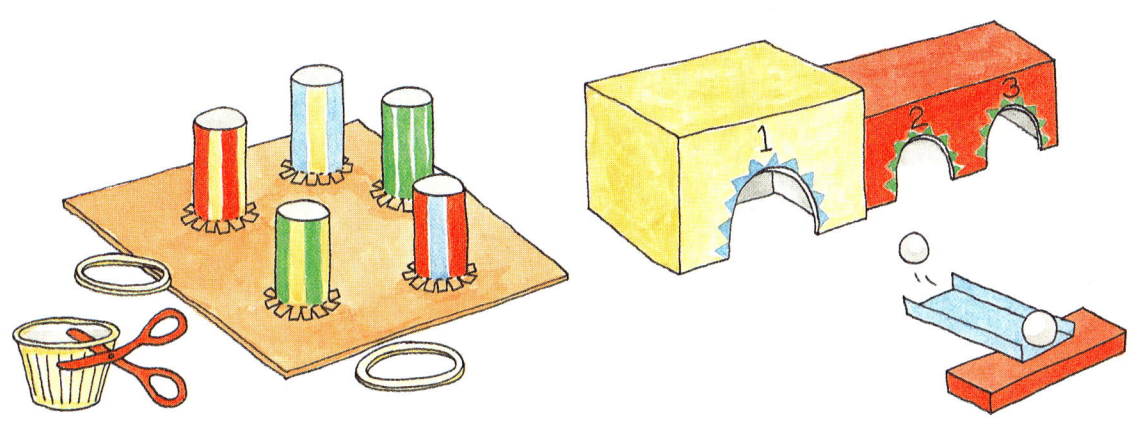

HODDER AND STOUGHTON
LONDON SYDNEY AUCKLAND TORONTO

To Chris, Catherine and Alex, for all their help.

British Library Cataloguing in Publication Data

Rice, Melanie
   Crafty ideas with junk.
   1. Handicrafts using scrap materials
   I. Title   II. Farmer, Lynne   III. Fairclough, Chris
745.584

   ISBN 0-340-52575-4

Text copyright © Melanie Rice 1991
Illustrations copyright © Lynne Farmer 1991

First published 1991

All rights reserved. No part of this publication may be reproduced or transmitted in any form or by any means, electronically or mechanically, including photocopying, recording, or any information storage and retrieval system, without either prior permission in writing from the publisher or a licence permitting restricted copying. In the United Kingdom such licences are issued by the Copyright Licensing Agency, 33-34 Alfred Place, London WC1E 7DP.

The rights of Melanie Rice to be identified as the author of the text of this work and of Lynne Farmer to be identified as the illustrator of this work have been asserted by them in accordance with the Copyright, Designs and Patents Act 1988.

Published by Hodder and Stoughton Children's Books, a division of Hodder and Stoughton Ltd, Mill Road, Dunton Green, Sevenoaks, Kent TN13 2YA

Design by Sally Boothroyd

Cover illustration by Lynn Breeze

Book list compiled by Peter Bone, Senior Librarian, Children's and Schools Services, Hampshire County Library

Printed in Great Britain by BPCC Hazell Books
Paulton, Bristol
Member of BPCC Ltd

CONTENTS

	Page
Notes to readers	4
Jangle dragon	6
Ostrich puppet	8
Photograph tree	10
Snowstorm	12
Boats	14
Space collage	16
Roundabout	18
Repeating patterns	20
Loons (Bottle puppets)	22
Jewellery	24
UFO mobile	26
Marble run	28
Book list	30
Index	31

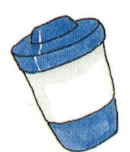 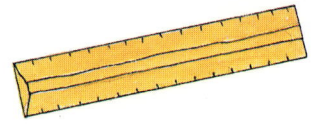  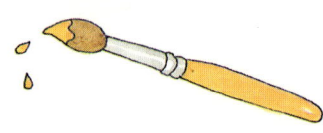

Note to parents and teachers

All the ideas in this book can easily be carried out at home or at school. Every item has been made by my own young children and then photographed for this book. Each page has clear instructions accompanied by numbered, easy-to-follow illustrations.

All the objects used here can be found at home: plastic bottles, cardboard cartons, buttons and beads etc.

PVA adhesive is a good all-round glue for use in model-making; its strength makes it ideal for sticking all materials.

Finding somewhere to leave finished items to dry can be a problem. It's best to put them on something which they will not stick to, such as a piece of plastic or wax paper. Some items can be hung up on a washing line!

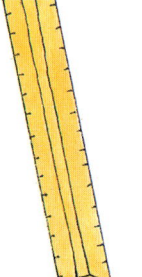
 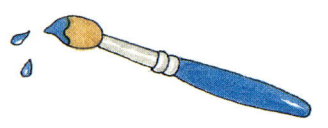  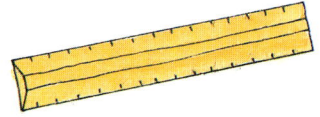

 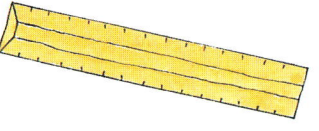  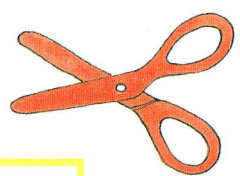

Note to children

Things to remember:

1. Read all instructions carefully before you begin so that you know what you have to do. Use the illustrations to help you.

2. Make sure everything you need is ready before you start.

3. Spread newspaper over your working surface – this is especially important for messy projects.

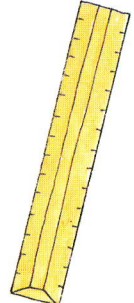

4. Clean up any mess after you have finished.

5. Put everything away tidily.

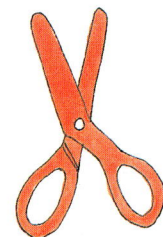

At the end of each project I have suggested more things for you to make. Maybe you have some ideas of your own. Don't be afraid to try them out.

Melanie Rice

  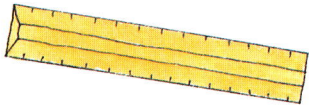 

JANGLE DRAGON

When carnival time arrives, you can be ready to celebrate with this jangly dragon.

You will need:

ball-point pen
thick material (60cm × 30cm)
needle
scissors
2 sticks
strong thread
collection of things that
 make different sounds

1 Draw a dragon about 60cm long on the material, and cut out as shown.

2 Using strong thread, tie or thread together the things you have collected. Some of the smaller items can be tied into net bags.

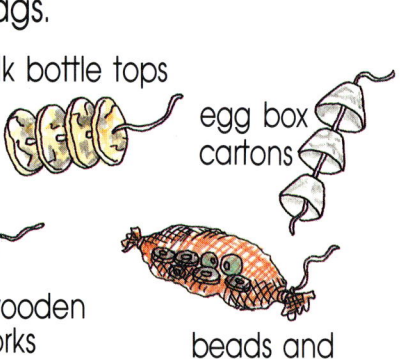

3 Stitch each thread firmly to one side of the dragon's body so that the strings of objects hang down.

4 Lay two sticks on the back of the material, one at the head, the other at the tail. Fold over 1cm of material along the top of the dragon and tuck the sticks into the fold. Stitch into place as shown.

Try making some shakers. You could use two yoghurt pots stuck together (with a pencil pushed into one end to make the handle), or plastic bottles with their lids firmly screwed on. Fill them with –

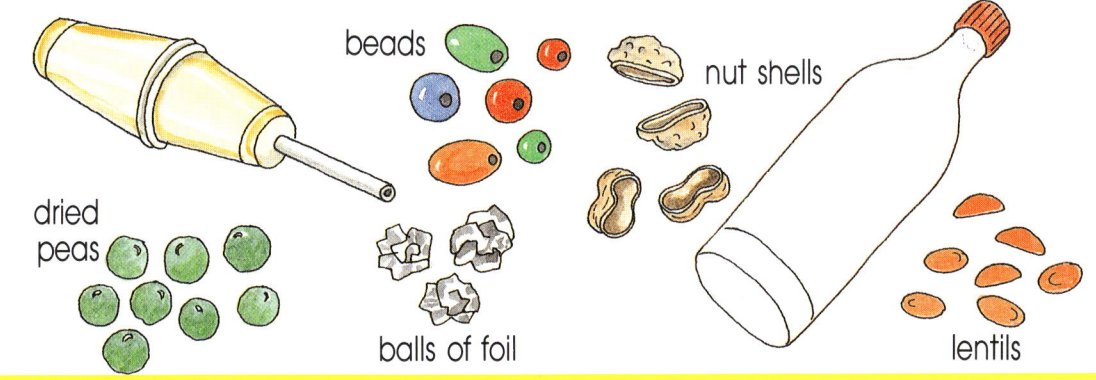

OSTRICH PUPPET

String puppets are easy to make, but harder to work. Practise with this ostrich, which has just two strings.

You will need:

1 large box
3 large buttons
1 large cardboard tube
3 small cardboard tubes
coloured paper
1 egg box
glue
paints
paint brush
1 piece of polystyrene
  (e.g. a meat tray)
scissors
string

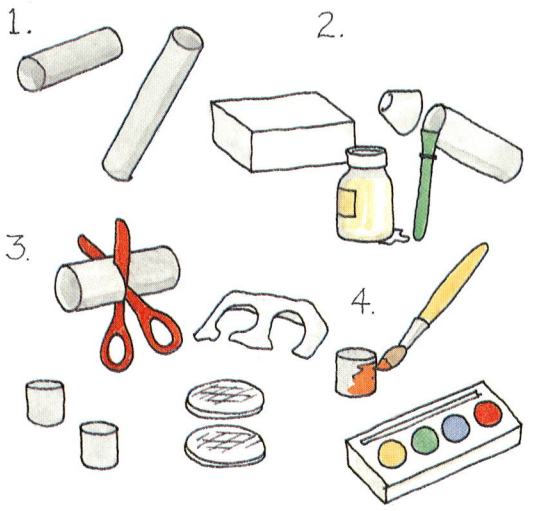

1 Use the large box for the body, the large tube for the neck, and one small tube for the head.

2 Cut out a piece of the egg carton. Glue it over one end of the small tube to make the beak. Paint two eyes on the head.

3 Cut the other two small tubes in half to make four rings. Then cut two circles from the polystyrene.

4 Paint or cover all the pieces with coloured paper.

5 To make a leg, tie a knot in a piece of string. Thread the other end through a button, through the middle of one polystyrene circle, through two of the cardboard rings and into the large box. Tie another knot to hold the leg in place. Repeat for the other leg.

6 Tie a knot in the third piece of string. Thread the other end through the third button, through the beak, the head and the neck and then tie to the body.

7 Stick on strips of coloured paper to make feathers and a tail.

8 Knot the ends of two more pieces of string. Thread one through the head and the other through the top of the body.

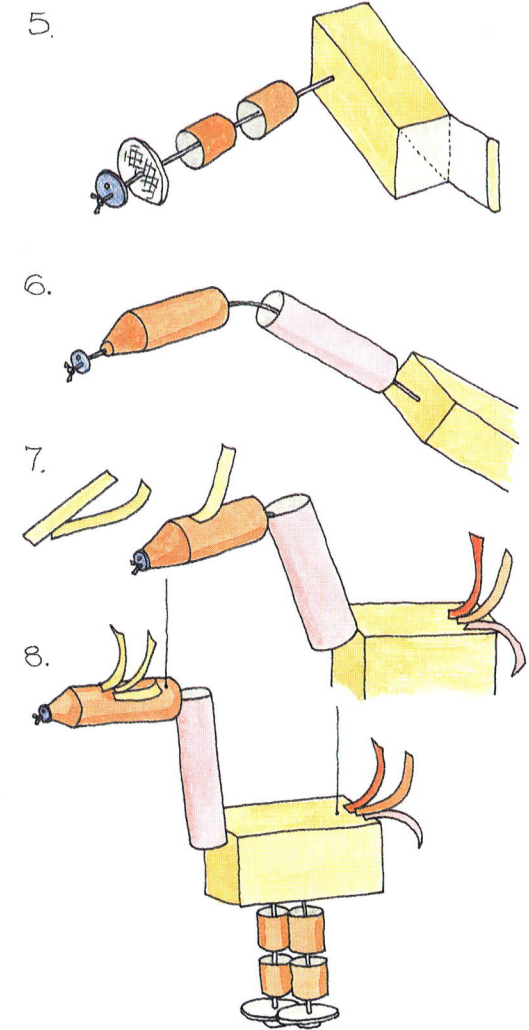

Here are some other string puppets you can make.

PHOTOGRAPH TREE

An illustrated family tree – keep it for yourself or give it as a birthday present to someone in your family.

You will need:

piece of cardboard
corrugated card
glue
net (e.g. supermarket
   vegetable bags)
green sugar paper
pieces of coloured tissue paper
family photographs
scissors

1 Cut the trunk and branches of the tree from corrugated card. Stick them on to the piece of cardboard.

2 Cut pieces of net to make bushy leaves. Stick them to the card.

3 Collect some photographs of members of your family (ask first). Cut out the heads and shoulders.

4 Cut a circle of tissue paper for each photograph. Pinch the middle of each so that it puckers slightly, then stick the photograph on to it.

5 Now glue each photograph on to your tree, putting the oldest members of your family at the top, and the youngest at the bottom.

6 Cut out small leaves from the sugar paper to stick round the photos.

Gift trees

Instead of cardboard, look for a real stick with several branches, then paint and press it into a plasticine base.

Now hang your photos from the branches.

For a tastier tree, use little bags of sweets instead of photos.

SNOWSTORM

Home-made snowstorms make fun presents for friends, and they put your old plastic toys to good use.

You will need:

kitchen foil
waterproof glue
1 jar with a screw-top lid
scissors
plastic toy (we used a knight)
washing-up liquid bottle

1.

a.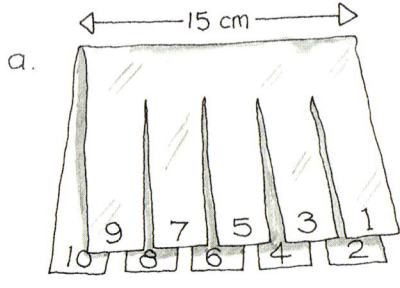

b.

c.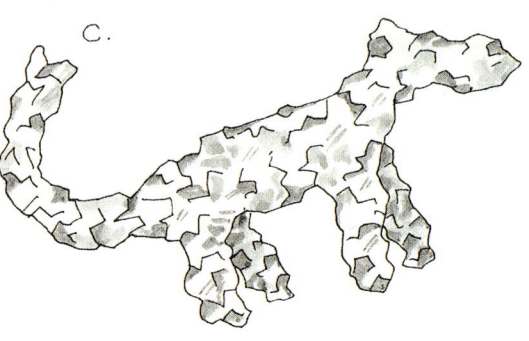

1 To make a foil dragon: fold a piece of kitchen foil in half. Make four cuts in it as shown. Twist pieces 1 and 2 to make a head, 3 and 4 to make the front legs, 5 and 6 to make the body, 7 and 8 to make the back legs, and 9 and 10 to make the tail.

2 Glue the foil model and the plastic toy to the bottom of the jar. Leave to dry.

3 To make the snowflakes: cut a section from the washing-up bottle into tiny pieces. Put the pieces into the jar.

4 Fill the jar to the top with water, then screw the lid on tightly. Shake the jar to make a snowstorm.

Other shapes you can make from foil

BOATS

Designing boats which actually float can be quite a challenge. Try this catamaran first, then add to your fleet using things you have at home. Be sure to make your boats from waterproof materials!

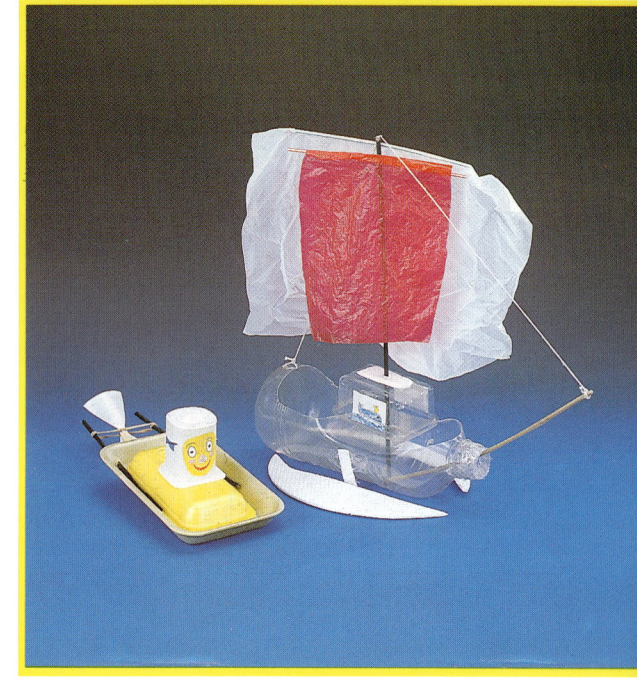

You will need:

1 elastic band
glue
1 lolly stick
1 plastic bag
1 plastic carton (e.g. from soft fruit)
1 large plastic squash bottle (3 litre)
1 polystyrene 'plate'
scissors
2 straws
3 sticks (canes)
string
1 yogurt pot or plastic cup

1 Cut the handle from the bottle, as shown.

2 Stick the plastic carton upside down on top of the bottle.

3 Make a hole through both and push a stick into the hole as the mast. Put another stick through the neck of the bottle as shown.

4 Break the third stick in half and push each half through the end of the bottle as shown. Glue all the sticks to the bottom of the bottle.

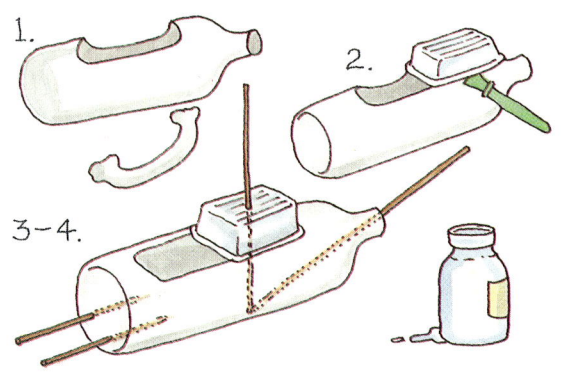

5. Make a small hole in the back end of the bottle. Knot a piece of string and thread the other end through the hole. Pull the piece of string to the top of the mast and glue it there, then tie the end to the front stick.

6. Cut two sails from the plastic bag. Stick one edge of each to a straw, then tie the straws to the mast.

7. Cut two triangles and two strips from the plastic cup.

8. Glue the triangles to the lolly stick to make a propeller. Leave to dry. Put the elastic band round the two sticks at the end of the boat and slip the propellor through the middle. Glue to the elastic band.

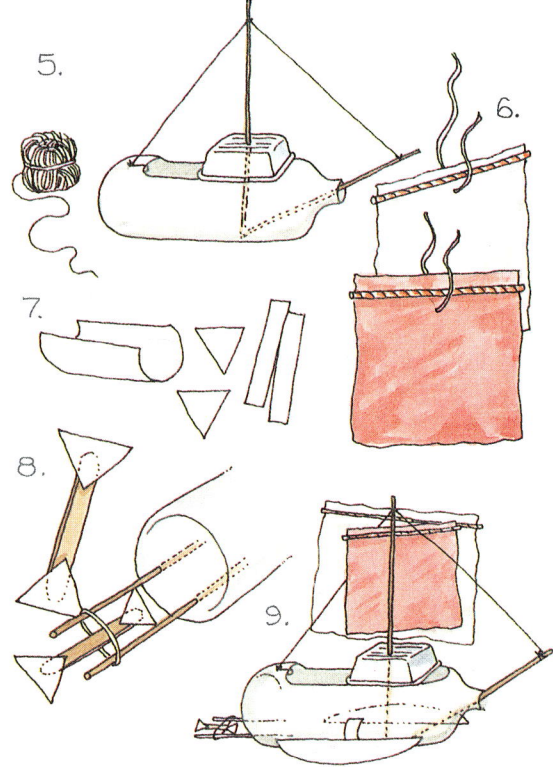

9. Cut out two crescents of polystyrene. Stick one end of each plastic strip to the side of the bottle, and the other end to a crescent, as shown.

Now try the following

junk   submarine   yacht

SPACE COLLAGE

You get two pictures for the price of one with this collage and rubbing. Put them on the wall and see if your friends spot the similarity.

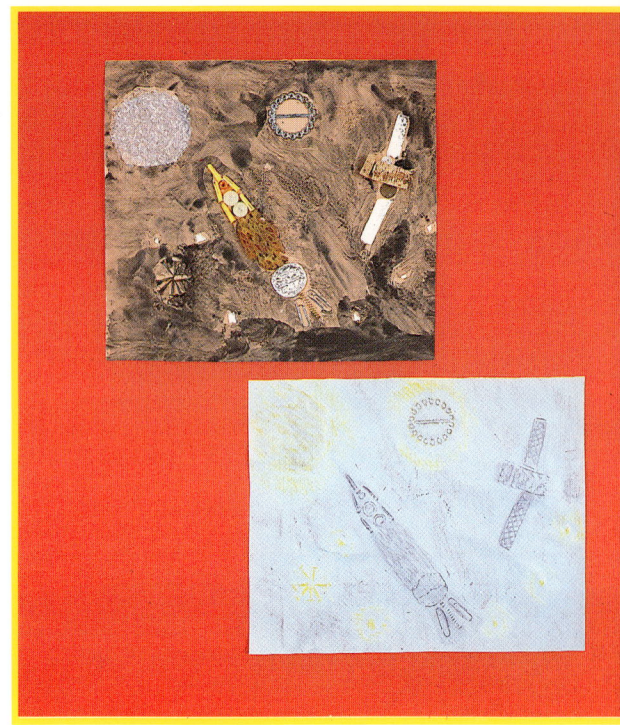

You will need:

glue
junk (e.g. a belt buckle)
buttons
1 cork
milk bottle top
nails
paper clips
plastic packaging
plastic wall plugs
polystyrene
2 pieces of paper
scissors
wax crayon

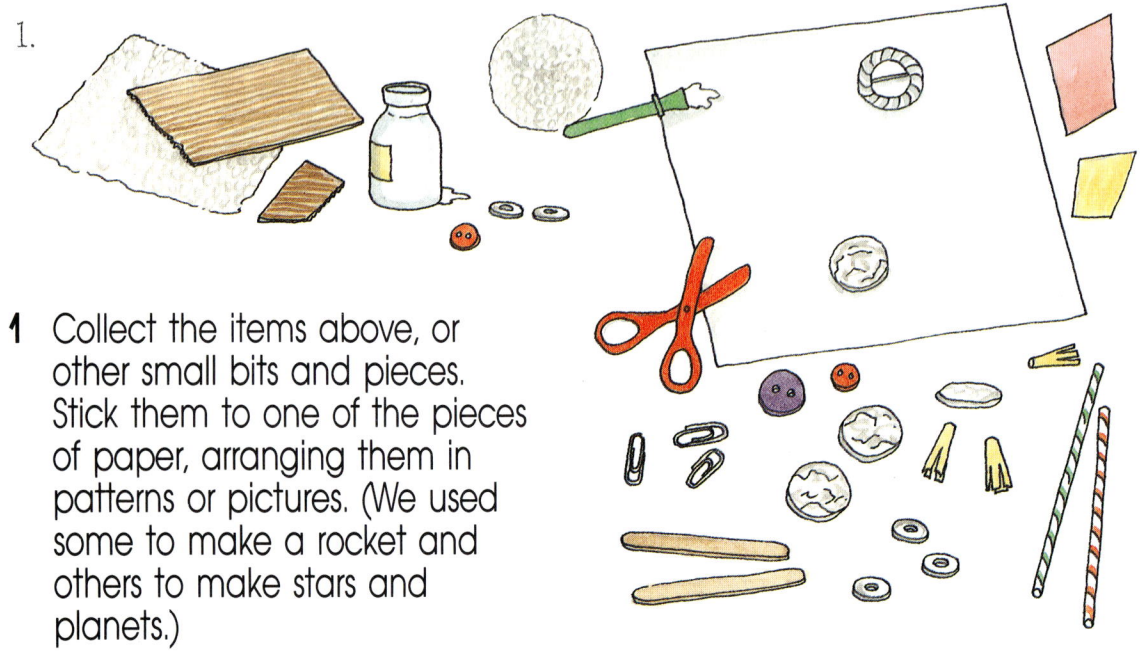

1.

1 Collect the items above, or other small bits and pieces. Stick them to one of the pieces of paper, arranging them in patterns or pictures. (We used some to make a rocket and others to make stars and planets.)

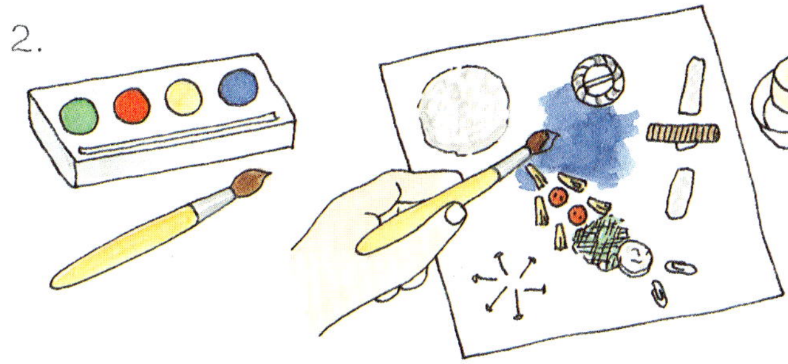

2 Paint over them, using a thin water colour.

3 When the glue and paint are dry, tape the other piece of paper over the top.

4 Rub wax crayons gently over the surface to make a rubbing of the collage.

5 Separate the two pieces of paper and you will have a collage and a rubbing for your wall.

Make a metallic plaque

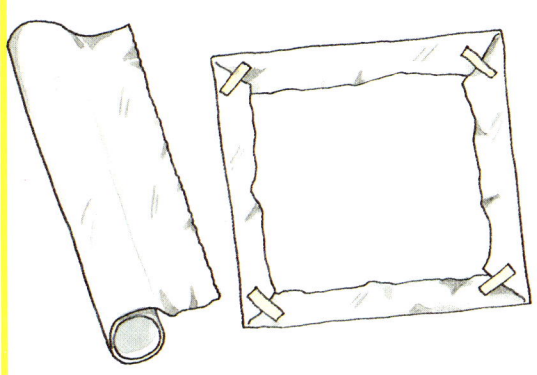

Cover the collage with a sheet of kitchen foil.

Then press the foil on to and around the objects.

ROUNDABOUT

Things that move are hard to make because you have to get the balance right, but this roundabout is quite simple and looks very effective.

You will need:

2 beads
1 bottle top
1 cardboard tube
lid from plastic tub
6 lolly sticks
4 plastic toys and 2 plastic boxes (film boxes)
round box (cheese box)
cotton thread
scissors
thin wire
empty spool (typewriter ribbon)

1 Cut slits evenly around the top and bottom of the cardboard tube. Fold them outwards, as shown, then glue one end of the tube to the round box and the other to the plastic lid.

2 Make a hole through the middle of the lid and another through the box.

3 Make a loop at one end of the wire, then thread the other end through the base, the tube and the circle of plastic.

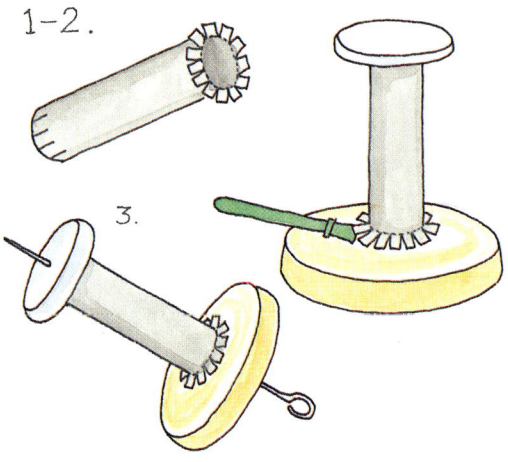

4 Continue threading the wire through the two beads and the spool.

5 Bend the top of the wire into a loop and cover with a bottle top.

4-5.

6 Glue the lolly sticks to the spool.

7 Make 'seats' by cutting plastic boxes, as shown, or find some light plastic toys.

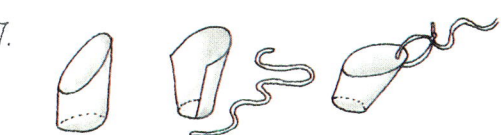

8 Tie the seats or toys to the lolly sticks with cotton thread, and spin round.

Creeping cotton reel

Thread an elastic band through a cotton reel, then put a matchstick through each end. (You can decorate the cotton reel if you like.)

Wind up the band by turning one matchstick.

Place the reel on the table and watch it creep along.

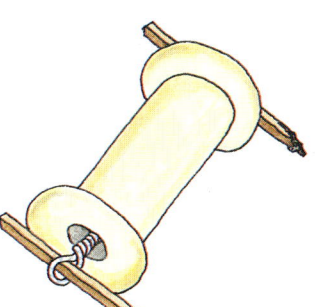
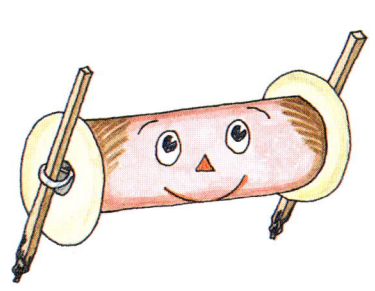

REPEATING PATTERNS

Islamic designs can be made by placing repeated shapes together. Fit them edge to edge and sometimes new shapes will appear in between.

You will need:

cardboard (cereal box)
coloured magazine
glue
paper
pencil
objects with interesting shapes
scissors

1 Make templates from part of a cardboard box by drawing around the shapes of some items found at home. We used a pastry cutter, an eraser, a plastic toy, and a cardboard box.

2 Cut out the shapes.

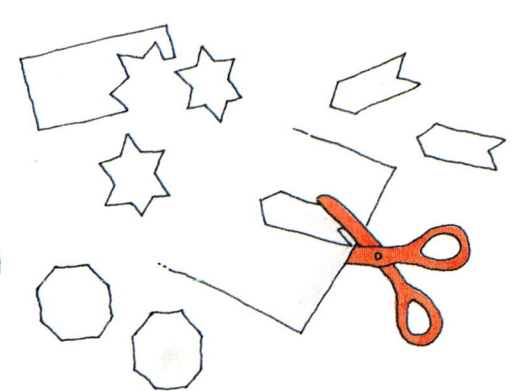

3 Place one of the templates on a page from a magazine. Draw around it. Then slide the shape along. Draw around it again and repeat 10 times.

4 Do the same thing again on a differently coloured page.

5 Cut the 12 shapes from one of the pages. Take the other page and cut out the areas in between.

6 Stick the pieces on to a piece of paper. Fit them neatly together without leaving any gaps.

Decorate pots for your room by sticking on sheets of shapes.

LOONS (BOTTLE PUPPETS)

These crazy puppets make good dancing partners. The foil in their heads rattles rhythmically as you swirl them around.

You will need:

2 buttons
chocolate box tray
1 cork
feathers
glue
scrap material
needle and thread
1 large plastic bottle (3 litre)
1 rectangular plastic tray
  (supermarket food container)
red net (fruit bag)
ribbons
scissors
wool

1 Turn the bottle upside down and cut three-quarters of the way round the top to make a lid.

2 Tie a knot at the end of a piece of strong thread or wool. Then thread together a button, and a piece of chocolate box tray to make an eye. Push the thread into the large bottle and out again as shown, then thread through the second tray and tie to the other button. Glue these pieces to the bottle to keep them firmly in place.

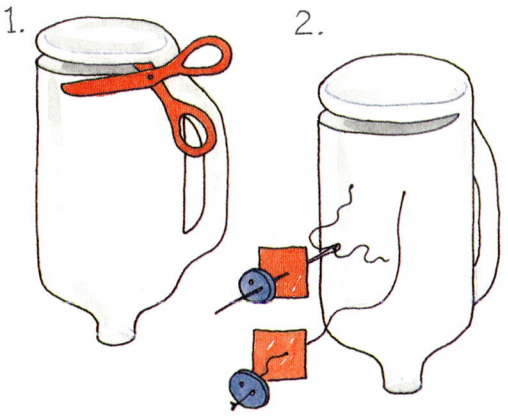

3 Cut a slit half-way round the bottom of the bottle. Fold the plastic food container in half, cover with the red net and push into the slit. Glue in place.

4 Cut a star into the bottle above the mouth and push the cork into it. Secure with glue.

5 Make six holes in the lid. Cut the wool into pieces, gather into three bunches, then tie to the top of the bottle through the holes, as shown.

6 Decorate by tying feathers and ribbons to the lid. Drop some milk bottle tops into the bottle, then close the lid with sticky tape.

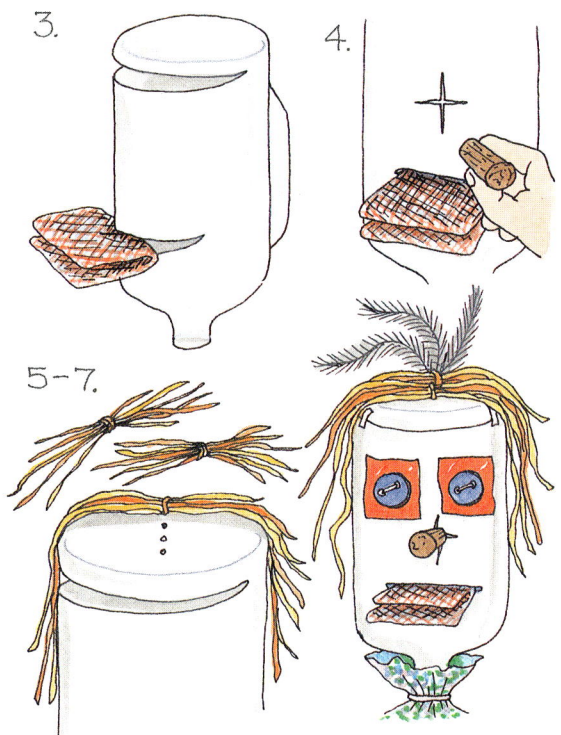

7 Tie a piece of material round the neck of the bottle to make a body.

Large plastic bottles can also be cut and made into masks.

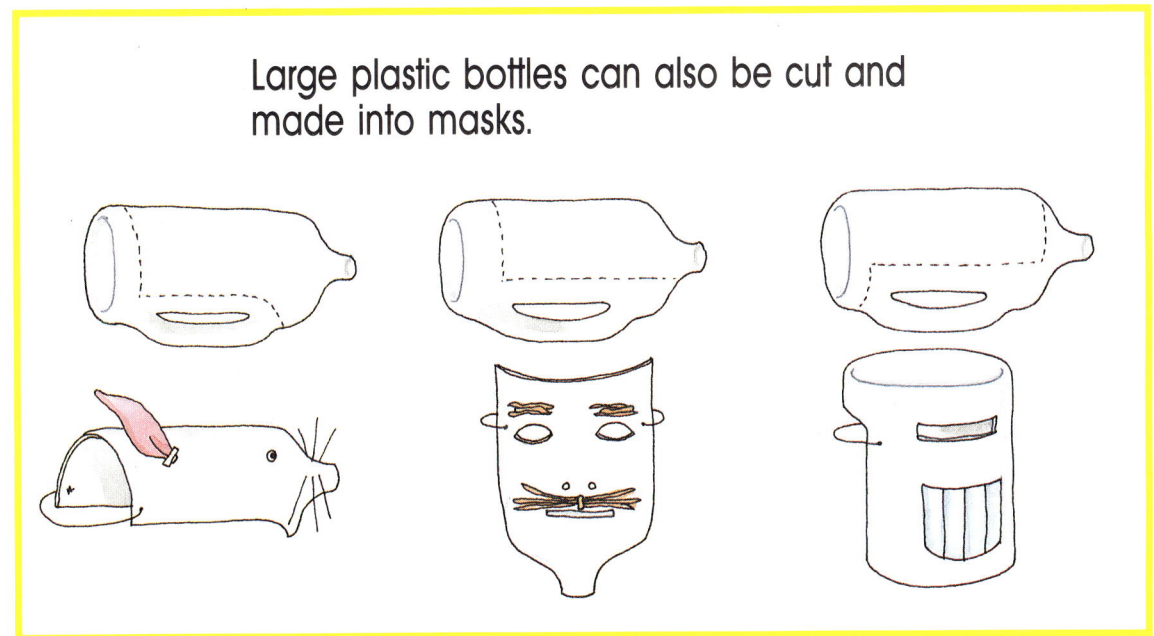

JEWELLERY

Dress yourself up for a party with your own home-made jewellery.

You will need:

1 small cardboard tube
cotton thread
knitting needle
paint brush
paints
thin paper
paste/glue
string
vaseline

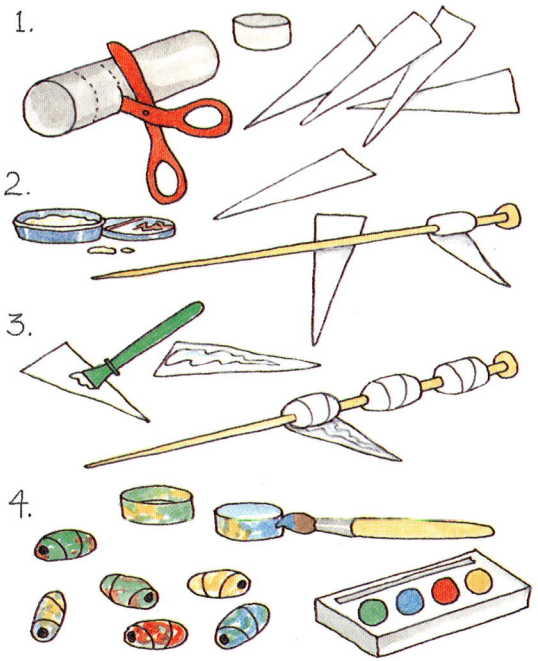

1 Cut the cardboard tube into rings and the paper into triangular strips, as shown.

2 Smooth a little vaseline over the needle.

3 To make the beads, brush the strips of paper with paste, then roll them around the needle, starting with the widest end each time. Leave to dry.

4 Remove the beads from the needle. Paint beads and rings in bright colours.

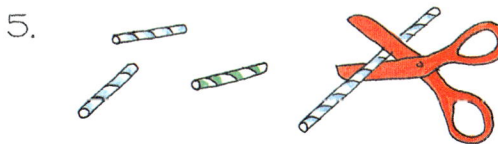

5 Cut a piece of straw to fit inside one of the rings. Do the same for the other rings.

6 Using thread, tie the straws into the rings then glue or tie the rings together.

7 Cut the string into three pieces. Plait them together, threading the beads into the plait, as shown.

8 Tie both ends of the plait to the rings.

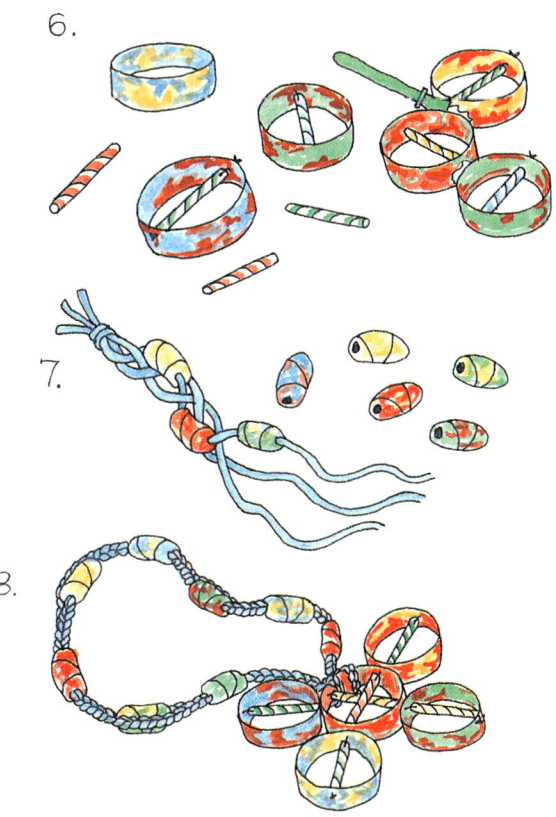

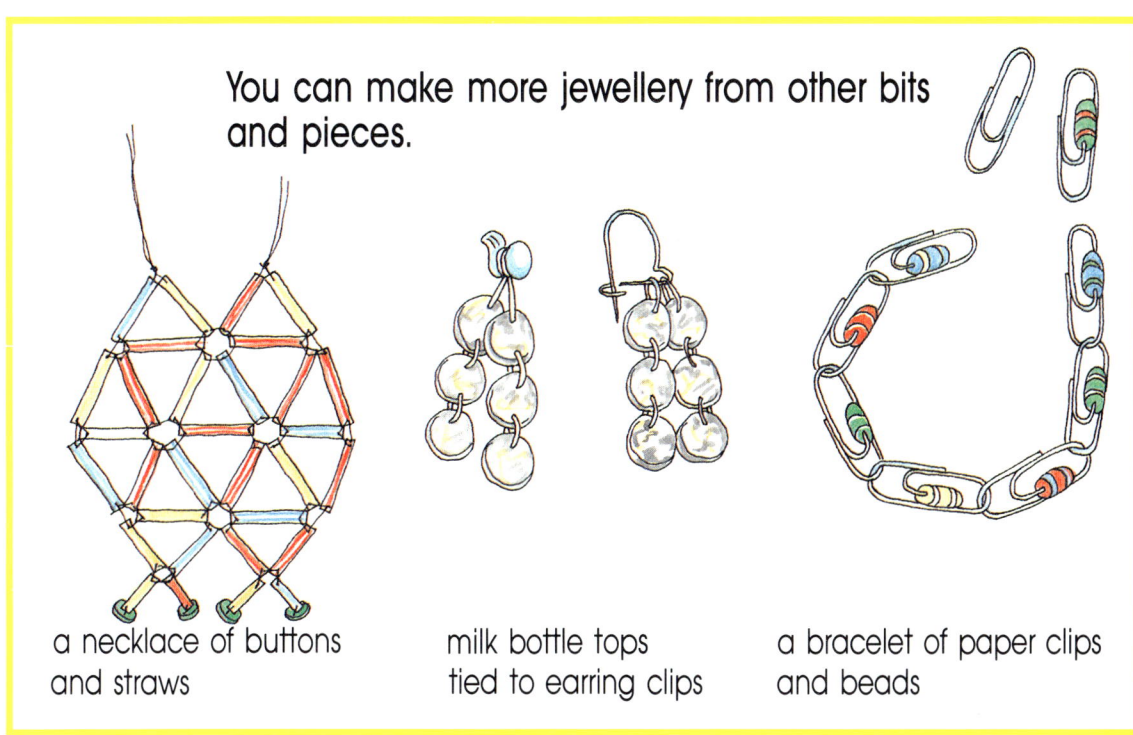

You can make more jewellery from other bits and pieces.

a necklace of buttons and straws

milk bottle tops tied to earring clips

a bracelet of paper clips and beads

UFO MOBILE

The Martians are coming! Brighten up your room with this colourful mobile.

You will need:

glue
lolly sticks
plastic or foil (fruit) pie tray
translucent coloured plastic
piece of polystyrene

2 sticks (30cm long)
straw
strong thread
table tennis ball
wire
large yoghurt pot

any of:
corks
cotton reels
milk bottle and plastic bottle tops
kitchen foil
cocktail sticks
beads

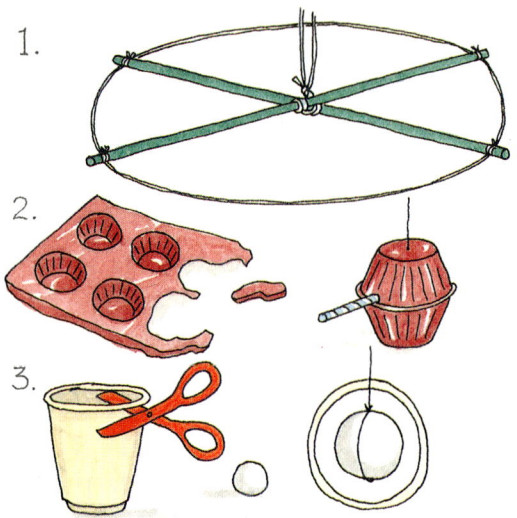

1. To make the frame: bind the two sticks together in the shape of a cross. Wind a circle of wire round them and tie in place. Now tie two pieces of thread to the middle of the cross for hanging the mobile.

2. To make the UFOs: cut out the segments from the plastic tray and stick two together. Push a straw into a small hole in the side.

3. Cut off the rim of the yoghurt pot. Glue a piece of thread around a table tennis ball and hang it from the middle of the rim.

4 Cut windows into the yoghurt pot, then stick coloured plastic inside to cover them. Push a straw through a hole in the bottom, then glue two lolly sticks to the straw as shown. Cover the top of the pot with a piece of plastic tray and hang upside down from the frame.

5 Cover corks and cotton reels with foil. Push cocktail sticks into them and glue beads on to the spiky ends. Add milk bottle tops and plastic bottle caps for decoration.

6 Cut out two circles from the polystyrene, then cut a slit into the middle of each. Slide the two pieces together as shown.

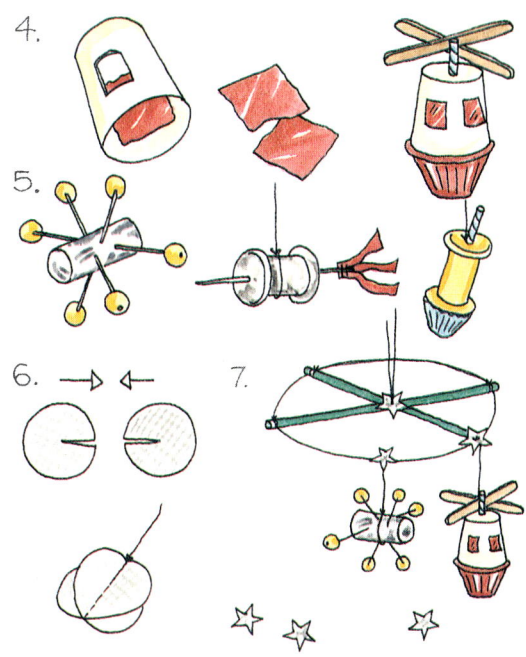

7 Hang all the UFOs from the frame, balancing them carefully. Glue on stars made from foil to hide the knots.

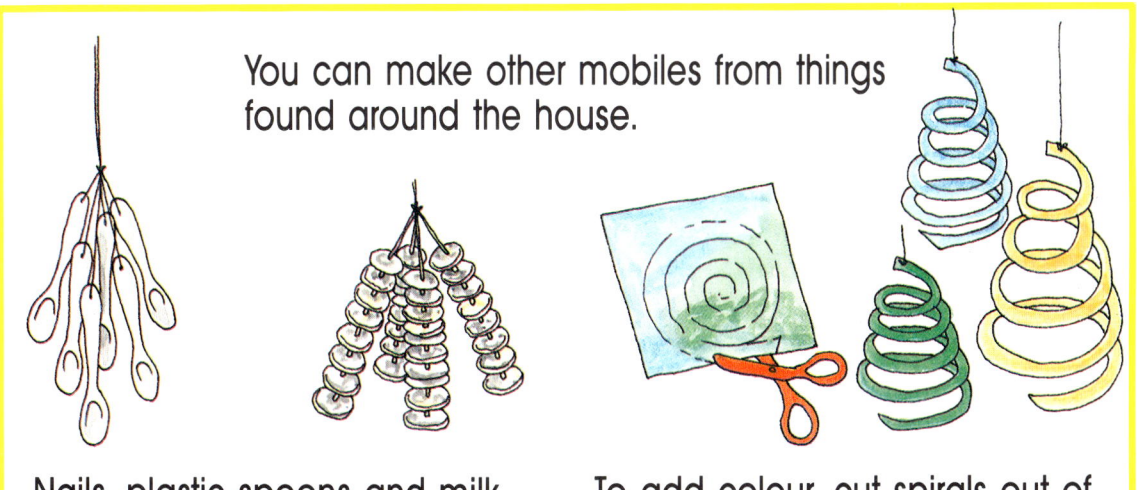

You can make other mobiles from things found around the house.

Nails, plastic spoons and milk bottle tops will jangle as they spin.

To add colour, cut spirals out of cardboard boxes and hang in clusters.

27

MARBLE RUN

Get your friends to guess the route the marble will take.

You will need:

large box (cereal)
smaller narrow boxes
  (e.g. toothpaste boxes)
  or cardboard tubes
glue
marble
paint
scissors

1.

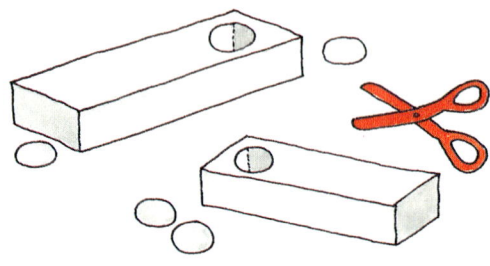

2.

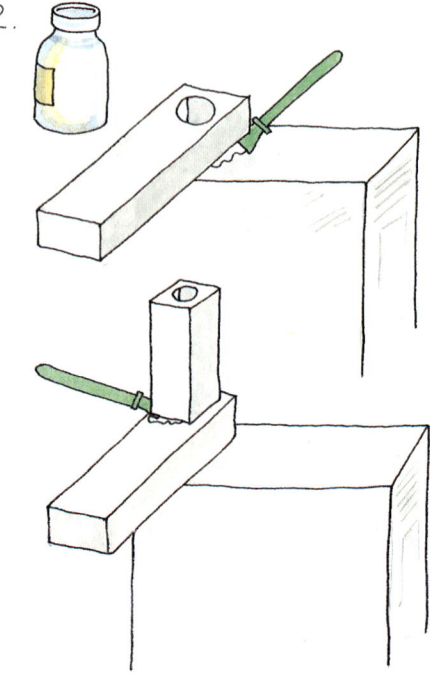

1 Cut a hole in the top and bottom of each narrow box as shown. (If you can't find enough boxes, use cardboard tubes instead.)

2 Glue one box to the top of the cereal packet, then glue a second box over the top hole.

3 Glue the other boxes to the sides of the cereal packet, one below the other, matching the holes. Tilt each one a little so that a marble will run down, dropping from box to box. Glue any spare boxes on at random to make it harder for people to guess which way the marble will roll.

4 Paint in bright colours.

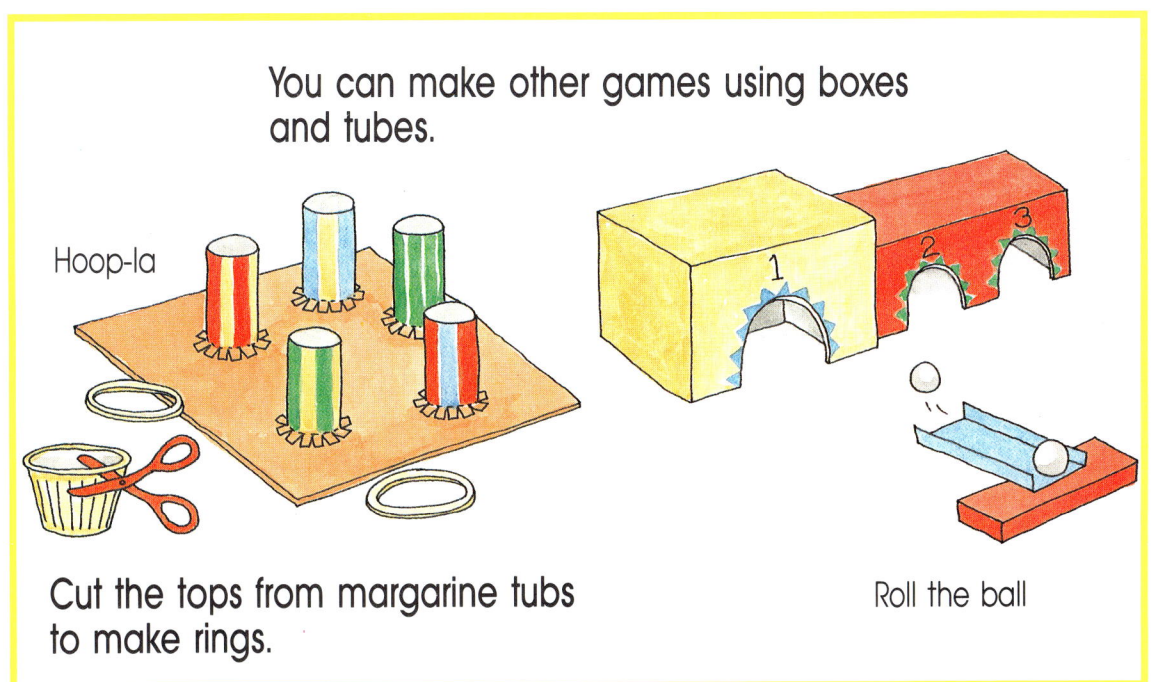

You can make other games using boxes and tubes.

Hoop-la

Cut the tops from margarine tubs to make rings.

Roll the ball

BOOK LIST

If you would like more ideas for things to make then the following books will help. Your local library should be able to get copies for you.

Caket, Colin.
MODEL A MONSTER: MAKING DINOSAURS FROM EVERYDAY MATERIALS.
Blandford Press, 1986. 0713716711
A great many ideas shown with clear line drawings, but not really a book for children to use by themselves.

Everett, Felicity.
MAKE YOUR OWN JEWELLERY.
Usborne, 1987. 0746000782
Bright and attractive book but with some complicated items of jewellery that will need adult help. There is a good section on using papier mâché.

Graham, Bob.
THE JUNK BOOK.
Blandford Press, 1986. 0713718595
A simple selection of ideas to recycle junk. The junk used includes tyres, timber and metal along with household items. No detailed descriptions given, just amusing illustrations and a few words to describe each activity.

Roussel, Mike.
SCRAP MATERIALS.
Wayland, 1989. 1852106727
Twelve ideas for projects using household junk such as plastic containers, polystyrene, cardboard packaging and paper. Easy to follow instructions.

West, Robin.
FAR OUT: HOW TO CREATE YOUR OWN STAR WORLD.
Carolrhoda books, 1987. 087614279X
How to make your own astro shuttle, cosmic centipede, meteor man and much more! Photographs of each project show what can be produced.

Wright, Lyndie.
PUPPETS.
Franklin Watts, 1988. 0863137431
Simple instructions and excellent photographs with some inspiring ideas for making your own puppets. Includes suggestions on how to make a puppet stage.

INDEX

beads 6, 7, 18, 19, 24, 25, 26, 27
bottles 12, 14, 15, 22-23
boxes 14, 18, 19, 20, 27, 28, 29

catamaran 14-15
collage 16-17
creeping cotton reel 19

dragons 6-7

fabric 6
foil 7, 12, 13, 17, 22, 26, 27

games 28-29
gift trees 11

Islamic designs 20-21

jewellery 24-25
junk (boat) 15

masks 23
mobiles 26-27
moving toy 19

photograph tree 10-11
plaque 17
puppets 22-23

roundabout 18-19

shaker 7
snowstorms 12-13
submarine 15

yacht 15